This guide is a gift from:

____

To : _______________________________

My prayer for you is that this season brings...

____

____

____

____

____

Karl Roussel

12 WEEKS TO 10X YOUR FAITH & CONTRIBUTION!

A Season Guided with **Daily** Questions, Prayer, and Verses to *Cultivate Spirit and Action* Through Trust, Knowledge, and Service!

1000X Kingdom

1000XFORTHEKINGDOM.COM

A word from the author: Karl Roussel

Dear reader, congratulations on your decision to draw closer to God and fulfill your potential!

I'll tell you why I created this guide for one season.
If God created the stars, the Sun and the Moon, it was to establish time and the seasons.

If this is God's creation and beneficial for nature, it is also beneficial for us, created in His image.
I was inspired by a call from God to create this guide, and I'm convinced that one of its purposes is to give us access to His Word every day.

He invites us to dialogue with Him daily, offering a way to make time for God in a fast-paced world.

Here are my wishes for your journey:

- That you connect more and more with your potential.
- That you recognize and value the talents God has given you to serve others.
- May it become a daily habit, and may you be inspired to continue with a next season, or even make it an annual habit.

But first, I'd like to...

May you enter into greater intimacy with God and Jesus, His only Son, who came to sacrifice Himself and wash away our sins with His blood.

May God bless you and may you spend blessed moments with Him, our Creator who loves us with great unconditional love.

John 3:16:
"For God loved the world so much that he gave his one and only Son, so that everyone who believes in him will not perish but have eternal life."

Karl Roussel

How to MAXIMI$€ this Prayer and Reflection Guide

Welcome to your 12-week spiritual journey!

1. Starts on a Saturday and then every Fourth Saturday: Four-Week Planning

Why Saturday? The guide starts on a Saturday to give you the opportunity to plan your first four-week block before you even begin.

Suggested time: 3 to 10 minutes

Action: Every fourth Saturday, take a moment to plan your next four weeks.
This will allow you to fully immerse yourself in the themes ahead and set personal goals.

2. Every Sunday: Prepare your Week

Suggested time: 3 to 10 minutes

Sunday Routine: Use every Sunday to plan the week ahead.
This will allow you to focus on the goals and prayers for the next few days.

3. Daily reading: Morning and Evening

Suggested time: Spend 3 to 10 minutes each morning reading, praying and answering questions.
In the evening, before going to bed, take another 3-5 minutes to reflect on your day.

Daily Routine: This regular practice is essential to build momentum and anchor these teachings in your daily life.

1000XFORTHEKINGDOM.COM/10Xfaith-contribution-bonus

4. Notes section : Personal reflection

Use the Notes section: Every day, in the notes section, write down your feelings after completing your readings and prayers.

How do you feel?

What changes are you seeing in your life?

Writing for Reflection: This step will enable you to see your progress and become aware of changes in your spiritual life.

5. Repetition and consistency

The Importance of Repetition: The aim is to repeat these steps from season to season. Incorporate these practices into your diary for the whole year, every year.

Build a Habit: By repeating these practices regularly, you'll build a solid habit of spiritual growth and development.

We wish you a rich and fulfilling journey with this guide.

May each page bring you closer to your faith, your contribution and your potential.

Published by: Profit Book Factory™ is a trademark of Oui c'est possible consultant INC.

First edition 2023

Published in Canada by Oui c'est possible consultant INC.

ISBN: 9798873354528

https://1000xforthekingdom.com/
Contact the author: info@karlroussel.com

1000XFORTHEKINGDOM.COM/10Xfaith-contribution-bonus

GO takes your bonuses:

__1000XFORTHEKINGDOM.COM/10Xfaith-contribution-bonus__

1000XFORTHEKINGDOM.COM/10Xfaith-contribution-bonus

Table of contents

INTENTION for your 12-week course with God?

Week 1-4 (Saturday 1): Foundations of Faith

Verse: Proverbs 3:5-6 - "Trust in the Lord with all your heart; do not depend on your own understanding. Seek his will in all you do, and he will show you which path to take."

Reflection Question: "What dimension of my faith would I like to deepen during these four weeks?"

____

____

Question to God: "What guidance or response do I hope to receive from God during this time?"

____

____

Prayer of Gratitude: "Lord, I thank You for having already answered my questions and guided my steps according to my intention. I am open to Your miraculous and surprising ways. Amen."

Notes for your next 4 weeks:

____

____

Week 1 (first Sunday): Trust in God

Verse: Psalm 37:5-6: "Surrender your life to the Lord, rely on him, and he will act. He will make your righteousness appear like light, and your justice like high noon."

Reflection Question: "How can I show my trust in God this week?"

____

____

Question to God: "In what aspect of my life do I need more clarity or trust in Your will?"

____

____

Prayer of Gratitude: "Thank You, Father, for clarifying my path and strengthening my trust in You. I am grateful for Your faithfulness and guidance. Amen."

Notes for your week:

____

____

Do you like presents? I've got some extras for you too, and a MEGA gift that I'll reveal at the end of your 12 weeks.

I invite you to pick up your bonuses at
1000XFORTHEKINGDOM.COM/10Xfaith-contribution-bonus

Monday - Strength and Confidence

Verse: Psalm 28:7 - "The Lord is my strength and shield. I trust him with all my heart. He helps me, and my heart is filled with joy. I burst out in songs of thanksgiving."

THANK YOU GOD FOR GIVING ME ANOTHER DAY!

Prayer: "Loving Father, You are my strength and my shield. Today, I place all my trust in You, knowing that You will rescue me. Fill my heart with joy and guide my steps in the celebration of Your goodness. Amen."

Reflection Question: "In what ways can I seek God's strength in my challenges today?"

____

____

BEFORE GOING TO BED!

Evening Review: "How have I experienced God's strength and support today?"

____

____

Thank You: "Thank You, Lord, for Your strength and presence in my life today."

Notes of the Day/Tomorrow:

____

____

Tuesday: Blessed in Trust

Verse: Jeremiah 17:7-8 - "But blessed are those who trust in the Lord and have made the Lord their hope and confidence. They are like trees planted along a riverbank, with roots that reach deep into the water. Such trees are not bothered by the heat or worried by long months of drought. Their leaves stay green, and they never stop producing fruit."

THANK YOU GOD FOR GIVING ME ANOTHER DAY!

Prayer: "Lord, I want to be like the tree planted by the waters, flourishing in every season thanks to my trust in You. Help me to remain firm and fruitful, even in difficult times, always relying on You. Amen."

Reflection Question: "How can I cultivate a deep trust in God in my daily life?"

BEFORE GOING TO BED!

Evening Review: "Where have I seen the blessings of trusting God today?"

Thanks: "Thank you, Father, for the peace and stability Your trust brings me."

Notes of the Day/Tomorrow:

Wednesday - Remission and Faith

Verse: Psalm 37:5 - "Commit everything you do to the Lord. Trust him, and he will help you."

THANK YOU GOD FOR GIVING ME ANOTHER DAY!

Prayer: "Heavenly Father, I entrust my life, my hopes and my worries to You. I have faith in Your providence and Your ability to act on my behalf. Guide my steps and open the ways before me, according to Your perfect will. Amen."

Reflection Question: "What aspects of my life should I hand over to God today?"

____

____

BEFORE GOING TO BED!

Evening Review: "How did I feel God's action in my life today?"

____

____

Thanks: "Thank You, Lord, for Your action and Your reassuring presence in my life."

Notes of the Day/Tomorrow:

____

____

Thursday -Focus on your Actions

Verse: Proverbs 16:3 - "Commit your actions to the Lord, and your plans will succeed."

THANK YOU GOD FOR GIVING ME ANOTHER DAY!

Prayer: "Lord, I place my plans and efforts in Your hands. Lead me in the realization of my plans, aligning my actions with Your will. May every step I take be blessed and fruitful under Your guidance. Amen."

Reflection Question: "How can I align my actions and projects with God's will?"

BEFORE GOING TO BED!

Evening Review: "Where did I see God guiding my actions and plans today?"

Thank You: "Thank You, Father, for the success and guidance You bring to my works."

Notes of the Day/Tomorrow:

Friday - Refuge and Trust

Verse: Psalm 62:8 - "O my people, trust in him at all times. Pour out your heart to him, for God is our refuge."

THANK YOU GOD FOR GIVING ME ANOTHER DAY!

Prayer: "Lord, You are my refuge and my strength. On this day, I pour out my heart to You, sharing my joys, fears and hopes. I find peace

and comfort in Your presence, knowing that You are always there for me. Amen."

Reflection Question: "How can I find comfort and peace in God today?"

____

____

BEFORE GOING TO BED!

Evening Review: "How have I experienced God as my refuge today?"

____

____

Giving thanks: "Thank you, Lord, for being my safe refuge and attentive listener."

Notes of the Day/Tomorrow:

____

____

Saturday - Protection and Faith

Verse: Psalm 91:2 - "This I declare about the Lord: He alone is my refuge, my place of safety; he is my God, and I trust him."

THANK YOU GOD FOR GIVING ME ANOTHER DAY!

Prayer: "Heavenly Father, You are my fortress and my refuge. In You I place my complete trust. Protect me and guide me through the challenges of this day. May I rest safely in Your loving care. Amen."

Reflection Question: "In what ways can I live today with full confidence in God's protection?"

BEFORE GOING TO BED!

Evening Review: "Where have I felt God's protection and security today?"

Thanks: "Thank You, Lord, for Your constant protection and unfailing love."

Notes of the Day/Tomorrow:

Sunday - Direction and Hope

Verse: Psalm 143:8 - "Let me hear of your unfailing love each morning, for I am trusting you. Show me where to walk, for I give myself to you."

THANK YOU GOD FOR GIVING ME ANOTHER DAY!

Prayer: "Lord, on this new day, I seek Your goodness and guidance. Show me the path I must follow, as my soul rises to You in trust and hope. Enlighten my decisions and actions with Your wisdom. Amen."

Reflection Question: "How can I open my heart to God's guidance first thing this morning?"

BEFORE GOING TO BED!

Evening Review: "How did I feel God's guidance and goodness today?"

Thank You: "Thank You, Father, for Your loving guidance and kindness every day."

Notes of the Day/Tomorrow:

Week 2 (Sunday 2): Divine Wisdom

Verse: James 1:5 - "If you need wisdom, ask our generous God, and he will give it to you. He will not rebuke you for asking."

Reflection Question: "In what area of my life do I need divine wisdom this week?"

Question to God: "What specific wisdom am I seeking from God during this week?"

Prayer of Gratitude: "Father, I thank You for the wisdom You generously pour into my life. I am ready to receive Your guidance and enlightenment. Amen."

Notes for your week:

PS: I don't know if you've seen my book that might interest you "Why 1000X, is EASIER than 10X & SIMPLER than 2X!" English and French version on AMAZON!

Monday - Source of Wisdom

Verse: Proverbs 2:6 - "For the Lord grants wisdom! From his mouth come knowledge and understanding."

THANK YOU GOD FOR GIVING ME ANOTHER DAY!

Prayer: "Lord, I recognize that all wisdom comes from You. Today, I ask for Your knowledge and intelligence to guide my decisions and actions. May I be a reflection of Your wisdom in this world. Amen."

Reflection Question: "How can I actively seek God's wisdom today?"

____

____

BEFORE GOING TO BED!

Evening Review: "How have I seen God's wisdom manifested in my life today?"

____

____

Thank You: "Thank You, God, for the wisdom You freely dispense."

Notes of the Day/Tomorrow:

____

____

Tuesday - Riches of Wisdom

Verse: Colossians 2:2-3 - "I want them to be encouraged and knit together by strong ties of love. I want them to have complete confidence that they understand God's mysterious plan, which is Christ himself. In him lie hidden all the treasures of wisdom and knowledge."

THANK YOU GOD FOR GIVING ME ANOTHER DAY!

Prayer: "Heavenly Father, I pray that my heart may be comforted and united in Your love. Help me to understand the riches of wisdom and knowledge found in Christ. May I discover the depths of Your mystery and truth. Amen."

Reflection Question: "How can wisdom and knowledge in Christ inspire me today?"

BEFORE GOING TO BED!

Evening Review: "Where have I felt the inspiration and consolation of Christ today?"

Thank You: "Thank You, Lord, for the treasures of wisdom and knowledge in You."

Notes of the Day/Tomorrow:

Wednesday - Advice and Wisdom

Verse: Proverbs 19:20 - "Get all the advice and instruction you can, so you will be wise the rest of your life."

THANK YOU GOD FOR GIVING ME ANOTHER DAY!

Prayer: "Lord, I pledge to listen attentively to advice and accept instruction. Guide me to the sources of wisdom that will enrich my life. May I grow in understanding and discernment at every step. Amen."

Reflection Question: "What advice or instructions should I look for or follow today?"

____

____

BEFORE GOING TO BED!

Evening Review: "How did I apply the wisdom I received today?"

____

____

Thanks: "Thank you, Father, for the advice and instructions that lead to wisdom."

Notes of the Day/Tomorrow:

____

____

Thursday - Spirit of Wisdom

Verse: Ephesians 1:17 - "Asking God, the glorious Father of our Lord Jesus Christ, to give you spiritual wisdom and insight so that you might grow in your knowledge of God."

THANK YOU GOD FOR GIVING ME ANOTHER DAY!

Prayer: "Father of glory, I humbly ask You to give me a spirit of wisdom and revelation. Open the eyes of my heart to fully understand Your will and Your truth. May I grow in the knowledge of You and Your love. Amen."

Reflection Question: "How can I open my heart to the spirit of wisdom and revelation today?"

____

____

BEFORE GOING TO BED!

Evening Review: "What did I learn new about God and His will today?"

____

____

Thank You: "Thank You, Lord, for the spirit of wisdom and revelation You offer me."

Notes of the Day/Tomorrow:

____

____

Friday - Priority to Wisdom

Verse: Proverbs 4:7 - "Getting wisdom is the wisest thing you can do! And whatever else you do, develop good judgment."

THANK YOU GOD FOR GIVING ME ANOTHER DAY!

Prayer: "Lord, I recognize that wisdom is the most precious thing. Help me to seek it and value it above all else. May I cultivate intelligence and understanding by relying on Your word and Your teaching. Amen."

Reflection Question: "How can I make acquiring wisdom a priority today?"

____

____

BEFORE GOING TO BED!

Evening Review: "In what ways have I sought and valued wisdom today?"

____

____

Thanks: "Thank you, God, for the priceless wealth of wisdom."

Notes of the Day/Tomorrow:

____

____

Saturday - Wisdom from Above

Verse: James 3:17 - "But the wisdom from above is first of all pure. It is also peace loving, gentle at all times, and willing to yield to others. It is full of mercy and the fruit of good deeds. It shows no favoritism and is always sincere."

THANK YOU GOD FOR GIVING ME ANOTHER DAY!

Prayer: "Heavenly Father, I desire the wisdom that comes from You, pure and peaceful. Fill my heart with Your wisdom, may my actions be moderate, conciliatory and full of mercy. May my life reflect the good fruits of Your divine wisdom. Amen."

Reflection Question: "How can I manifest divine wisdom in my interactions today?"

BEFORE GOING TO BED!

Evening Review: "How have I applied wisdom from on high in my life today?"

Thanks: "Thank You, Lord, for the purity and peace of Your wisdom."

Notes of the Day/Tomorrow:

Sunday - Foundation of Wisdom

Verse: Psalm 111:10 - "Fear of the Lord is the foundation of true wisdom. All who obey his commandments will grow in wisdom. Praise him forever!"

THANK YOU GOD FOR GIVING ME ANOTHER DAY!

Prayer: "Lord, I recognize that fearing You is the foundation of all wisdom. Help me to live in respect and reverence for You. May my life be a testimony to Your greatness and power, and may I always remain in the way of wisdom. Amen."

Reflection Question: "How can the fear of the Lord point me toward deeper wisdom?"

BEFORE GOING TO BED!

Evening Review: "How have I experienced the wisdom that comes from fearing the Lord today?"

Thank You: "Thank You, Father, for the wisdom that comes from fearing and respecting You."

Notes of the Day/Tomorrow:

Week 3 (Sunday 3): Grace and Blessing

Verse: 2 Corinthians 9:8 - "And God will generously provide all you need. Then you will always have everything you need and plenty left over to share with others."

Reflection Question: "What graces and blessings do I hope to receive and recognize this week?"

____

____

Question to God: "What particular blessing would I like to ask God for this week?"

____

____

Prayer of Gratitude: "Father, I thank You for the abundant graces and blessings You have prepared for me. I am open and grateful for Your generosity. Amen."

Notes for your week:

____

____

Do you like presents? I've got some extras for you too, and a MEGA gift that I'll reveal at the end of your 12 weeks.

I invite you to pick up your bonuses at 1000XFORTHEKINGDOM.COM/10Xfaith-contribution-bonus

Monday - Gift of Grace

Verse: Ephesians 2:8 - "God saved you by his grace when you believed. And you can't take credit for this; it is a gift from God."

THANK YOU GOD FOR GIVING ME ANOTHER DAY!

Prayer: "Lord, I am deeply grateful for the undeserved gift of Your saving grace. Help me to live in full recognition of this gift, resting in faith and trust in You. Amen."

Reflection Question: "How can I express my gratitude for the gift of grace today?"

____

____

BEFORE GOING TO BED!

Evening Review: "How have I experienced God's saving grace today?"

____

____

Thank You: "Thank You, God, for Your incredible gift of grace."

Notes of the Day/Tomorrow:

____

____

Tuesday - Providence and Care

Verse: Psalm 23:1 - "The Lord is my shepherd; I have all that I need."

THANK YOU GOD FOR GIVING ME ANOTHER DAY!

Prayer: "Loving Father, You are my shepherd and in Your care I lack nothing. I trust in Your providence and care for all my needs. May I rest in peace, knowing that You provide for my needs. Amen."

Reflection Question: "How can I rest in God's providence today?"

____

____

BEFORE GOING TO BED!

Evening Review: "Where have I seen God's providential hand in my life today?"

____

____

Thank You: "Thank You, Lord, for Your constant providence and care."

Notes of the Day/Tomorrow:

____

____

Wednesday - Comfort in mourning

Verse: Matthew 5:4 - "God blesses those who mourn, for they will be comforted."

THANK YOU GOD FOR GIVING ME ANOTHER DAY!

Prayer: "Lord, in my moments of sadness and grief, I turn to You for comfort. Fill my heart with Your comfort and love. May I find peace and hope in Your welcoming arms. Amen."

Reflection Question: "How can I seek God's comfort in my time of need?"

BEFORE GOING TO BED!

Evening Review: "How have I felt God's consolation in my moments of sadness?"

Thank You: "Thank You, God, for the blessing of Your comfort and consolation."

Notes of the Day/Tomorrow:

Thursday - Blessing and Favor

Verse: Psalm 84:11 - "For the Lord God is our sun and our shield. He gives us grace and glory. The Lord will withhold no good thing from those who do what is right."

THANK YOU GOD FOR GIVING ME ANOTHER DAY!

Prayer: "Father, You are my sun and my shield. I thank You for the graces and blessings You pour into my life. Help me to walk in integrity so that I may receive all the goods You have in store for me. Amen."

Reflection Question: "In what ways can I walk in integrity to receive God's blessings?"

BEFORE GOING TO BED!

Evening Review: "Where have I seen God's grace and favor manifested today?"

Thank You: "Thank You, Lord, for Your grace and favor in my life."

Notes of the Day/Tomorrow:

Friday - Abundance of Blessings

Verse: Psalm 67:7 - "Yes, God will bless us, and people all over the world will fear him."

THANK YOU GOD FOR GIVING ME ANOTHER DAY!

Prayer: "Lord, I thank You for the abundant blessings You shower on my life. May Your generosity guide me to live in awe and adoration of You, and may Your goodness be known through me in the world. Amen."

Reflection Question: "How can I reflect the abundance of God's blessings in my life?"

____

____

BEFORE GOING TO BED!

Evening Review: "In what ways have I shared and celebrated God's blessings today?"

____

____

Thank You: "Thank You, Father, for Your boundless generosity and grace in my life."

Notes of the Day/Tomorrow:

____

____

Saturday - Priestly blessing

Verse: Numbers 6:24-26 - "May the Lord bless you and protect you. May the Lord smile on you and be gracious to you. May the Lord show you his favor and give you his peace."

THANK YOU GOD FOR GIVING ME ANOTHER DAY!

Prayer: "Almighty God, I gratefully receive Your priestly blessing. May Your peace, grace and protection be upon me and all around me. May Your light shine in my life, bringing harmony and well-being. Amen."

Reflection Question: "How can I be a channel of God's blessing and peace?"

BEFORE GOING TO BED!

Evening Review: "Where have I felt or shared God's peace and grace today?"

Thank You: "Thank You, Lord, for Your blessing and peace that surpass all understanding."

Notes of the Day/Tomorrow:

Sunday - Blessing of the Work

Verse: Psalm 90:17 - "And may the Lord our God show us his approval and make our efforts successful. Yes, make our efforts successful!"

THANK YOU GOD FOR GIVING ME ANOTHER DAY!

Prayer: "Heavenly Father, may Your grace be upon me and all that I undertake. Strengthen the work of my hands, so that my actions and efforts reflect Your goodness and contribute to Your kingdom. May each day be a testimony of Your faithfulness. Amen."

Reflection Question: "How can I collaborate with God to strengthen the work of my hands?"

BEFORE GOING TO BED!

Evening Review: "How have I seen the work of my hands blessed and strengthened by God today?"

Thanks: "Thank You, Lord, for Your hand that guides and strengthens my work."

Notes of the Day/Tomorrow:

Week 4 (Sunday 4): Faith and Action

Verse: James 2:17 - "So you see, faith by itself isn't enough. Unless it produces good deeds, it is dead and useless."

Reflection Question: "What actions can I take this week to demonstrate my faith?"

Question to God: "What opportunities for faithful action will you reveal to me this week?"

Prayer of Gratitude: "Father, I thank You for the living faith You nourish in me and for the opportunities to act according to Your will. May my actions reflect my faith in You. Amen."

Notes for your week:

PS: I don't know if you've seen my book that might interest you "Why 1000X, is EASIER than 10X & SIMPLER than 2X!" English and French version on AMAZON!

Monday - Faith that Moves Mountains

Verse: Matthew 17:20 - "You don't have enough faith," Jesus told them. "I tell you the truth, if you had faith even as small as a mustard seed, you could say to this mountain, 'Move from here to there,' and it would move. Nothing would be impossible."

THANK YOU GOD FOR GIVING ME ANOTHER DAY!

Prayer: "Lord, give me faith as small as a mustard seed to see the impossible become possible. Help me to trust in Your power and to act with confidence, knowing that You are with me. Amen."

Reflection Question: "What 'mountain' can I tackle with faith today?"

____

____

BEFORE GOING TO BED!

Evening Review: "How have I used my faith to face today's challenges?"

____

____

Thanks: "Thank you, Father, for the strength my faith in You brings me."

Notes of the Day/Tomorrow:

____

____

Tuesday - Walking in Faith

Verse: 2 Corinthians 5:7 - "For we live by believing and not by seeing."

THANK YOU GOD FOR GIVING ME ANOTHER DAY!

Prayer: "Almighty God, help me to walk by faith and not by what I see. Let my trust in You guide my steps each day. Even in uncertainty, may I be assured of Your presence and Your plan. Amen."

Reflection Question: "How can I practice active faith in my daily life?"

____

____

BEFORE GOING TO BED!

Evening Review: "In what moments have I chosen to walk by faith rather than by sight?"

____

____

Thanks: "Thank you, Lord, for the clarity and direction that faith brings me."

Notes of the Day/Tomorrow:

____

____

Wednesday - Faith Working Through Love

Verse: Galatians 5:6 - "When we place our faith in Christ Jesus, there is no benefit in being circumcised or being uncircumcised. What is important is faith expressing itself in love."

THANK YOU GOD FOR GIVING ME ANOTHER DAY!

Prayer: "Father, may my faith always be active in love. May my actions reflect Your compassion and grace. In my relationships and commitments, may love be the driving force of my faith. Amen."

Reflection Question: "How can I manifest love in my faith actions today?"

BEFORE GOING TO BED!

Evening Review: "How have I witnessed faith through love in my day?"

Thanksgiving: "Thank you, God, for the ability to live an active faith through love."

Notes of the Day/Tomorrow:

Thursday - Faith and Prayer

Verse: Mark 11:22-24 - "Then Jesus said to the disciples, 'Have faith in God. I tell you the truth, you can say to this mountain, 'May you be lifted up and thrown into the sea,' and it will happen. But you must really believe it will happen and have no doubt in your heart. I tell you, you can pray for anything, and if you believe that you've received it, it will be yours.'"

THANK YOU GOD FOR GIVING ME ANOTHER DAY!

Prayer: "Lord, strengthen my faith so that my prayers are filled with total trust in You. Help me to firmly believe that You are capable of achieving the impossible. May my words and actions reflect this unshakeable faith. Amen."

Reflection Question: "How can my prayer today reflect unwavering faith?"

BEFORE GOING TO BED!

Evening Review: "How has my faith influenced my prayers and actions today?"

Thanks: "Thank you, Father, for the power of prayer and the certainty of faith."

Notes of the Day/Tomorrow:

Friday - Substance of Faith

Verse: Hebrews 11:1 - "Faith is the confidence that what we hope for will actually happen; it gives us assurance about things we cannot see."

THANK YOU GOD FOR GIVING ME ANOTHER DAY!

Prayer: "Heavenly Father, may my faith be the firm assurance of my hopes, the proof of the invisible. Help me to remain constant in faith, even when circumstances seem uncertain. May my life be a living testimony to this assurance. Amen."

Reflection Question: "How can I live today with firm assurance in what I hope for?"

BEFORE GOING TO BED!

Evening Review: "In what moments did I feel the strength of my faith today?"

Thanks: "Thank you, Lord, for the firm assurance that faith brings me."

Notes of the Day/Tomorrow:

Who do you think would find this book helpful and need to connect with God?

Know someone with untapped potential and God-given talents?

This book could be the key to unlocking their true capabilities.

Share it with them and help illuminate the path to their spiritual and personal growth.

____

____

____

____

____

____

https://1000xforthekingdom.com/12-weeks-10xfaith-and-contribution

Share the joy and connection with God with those people!

Saturday - Faith through Acts

Verse: 1 John 3:18 - "Dear children, let's not merely say that we love each other; let us show the truth by our actions."

THANK YOU GOD FOR GIVING ME ANOTHER DAY!

Prayer: "Lord, help me to live my faith not just in words, but in concrete, sincere deeds. May my love for You and for my neighbor manifest itself in my daily actions, bearing witness to Your truth and Your grace. Amen."

Reflection Question: "What concrete actions can I take today to demonstrate my faith?"

____

____

BEFORE GOING TO BED!

Evening Review: "How have my actions today been a reflection of my faith?"

____

____

Thanksgiving: "Thank you, God, for the opportunity to live out my faith through acts of love and truth."

Notes of the Day/Tomorrow:

____

____

Week 5-8 (Saturday 5): Vision and Goals

Verse: Proverbs 29:18 - "When people do not accept divine guidance, they run wild. But whoever obeys the law is joyful."

Reflection Question: "What clear vision would I like to develop for my life over these next four weeks?"

____

____

Question to God: "What specific guidance am I seeking from God to clarify my vision and goals?"

____

____

Gratitude Prayer: "Lord, thank You in advance for the clarity and direction You will provide, to help me refine my vision and achieve my goals. I have faith in Your guidance. Amen."

What's your greatest achievement in the last 4 weeks? (I invite you to share it on social media by tagging me @KarlRoussel)

____

____

Notes for the next 4 weeks:

____

____

Sunday - Necessity of Faith

Verse: Hebrews 11:6 - "And it is impossible to please God without faith. Anyone who wants to come to him must believe that God exists and that he rewards those who sincerely seek him."

THANK YOU GOD FOR GIVING ME ANOTHER DAY!

Prayer: "Eternal Father, I believe in Your presence and in Your reward for those who seek You. Strengthen my faith so that I may always be pleasing to You and follow You with all my heart. May my search for You be sincere and persevering. Amen."

Reflection Question: "How can I seek God with sincere, persevering faith today?"

____

____

BEFORE GOING TO BED!

Evening Review: "How has my faith brought me closer to God today?"

____

____

Thank You: "Thank You, Lord, for the promise of Your presence and Your reward for my faith."

Notes of the Day/Tomorrow:

____

____

Week 5 (Sunday 5): Clear vision

Verse: Jeremiah 29:11: "For I know the plans I have for you," says the Lord. "They are plans for good and not for disaster, to give you a future and a hope."

Reflection Question: "How can I apply my clear vision to my daily actions this week?"

____

____

Question to God: "What concrete steps can I take this week to move toward realizing my vision?"

____

____

Prayer of Gratitude: "Father, I thank You for the wisdom and enlightenment You offer me to realize my vision. Guide me every step of the way. Amen."

Notes for the week ahead:

____

____

PS: I don't know if you've seen my book that might interest you "Why 1000X, is EASIER than 10X & SIMPLER than 2X!" English and French version on AMAZON!

1000XFORTHEKINGDOM.COM/10Xfaith-contribution-bonus

Monday - Writing the Vision

Verse: Habakuk 2:2 - "Then the Lord said to me, 'Write my answer plainly on tablets, so that a runner can carry the correct message to others.'"

THANK YOU GOD FOR GIVING ME ANOTHER DAY!

Prayer: "Lord, inspire me to write down clearly the vision You have placed in my heart. May I share it with conviction and enthusiasm, motivating myself and others to act with faith and determination. Amen."

Reflection Question/Collaboration with God: "How can I realize and communicate my vision today?"

____

____

BEFORE GOING TO BED!

Evening Review: "How did I share or work on my vision today?"

____

____

Thank You: "Thank You, Father, for the clarity of vision You have given me."

Notes for today or tomorrow:

____

____

Tuesday - Enlightenment of the Spirit

Verse: Ephesians 1:18 -"I pray that your hearts will be flooded with light so that you can understand the confident hope he has given to those he called—his holy people who are his rich and glorious inheritance."

THANK YOU GOD FOR GIVING ME ANOTHER DAY!

Prayer: "Lord, enlighten the eyes of my heart with Your Spirit. Help me to fully understand the hope and richness of Your call. May my vision be aligned with Your will and may I discern my path clearly. Amen."

Reflection Question/Collaboration with God: "How can spiritual enlightenment influence my vision today?"

BEFORE GOING TO BED!

Evening Review: "In what areas have I felt the Spirit's illumination and guidance today?"

Thank You: "Thank You, God, for the spiritual enlightenment You bring to my life."

Notes for today or tomorrow:

Wednesday - Cooperating with God

Verse: Proverbs 16:9 -"We can make our plans, but the Lord determines our steps."

THANK YOU GOD FOR GIVING ME ANOTHER DAY!

Prayer: "Father, as I plan my route, I entrust the direction of my steps to You. Help me to cooperate with Your perfect plans, knowing that You are leading me to the best path. May my vision be in harmony with Your will. Amen."

Reflection Question/Collaboration with God: "In what ways can I align my plans with God's direction today?"

____

____

BEFORE GOING TO BED!

Evening Review: "How did I see God directing my steps today?"

____

____

Thank You: "Thank You, Lord, for Your guidance and wisdom in my life."

Notes for today or tomorrow:

____

____

Thursday - The Word as Guide

Verse: Psalm 119:105 - "Your word is a lamp to guide my feet and a light for my path."

THANK YOU GOD FOR GIVING ME ANOTHER DAY!

Prayer: "Lord, may Your Word be the light that guides my path. In every decision and every action, may I be guided by Your teachings and wisdom. May my vision be illuminated by Your truth. Amen."

Reflection Question/Collaboration with God: "How can God's Word inform my vision today?"

____

____

BEFORE GOING TO BED!

Evening Review: "How have I used God's Word as a guide today?"

____

____

Thanks: "Thank You, Father, for Your Word which enlightens my path."

Notes for today or tomorrow:

____

____

Friday - Tips and Plans

Verse: Proverbs 15:22 - "Plans go wrong for lack of advice; many advisers bring success."

THANK YOU GOD FOR GIVING ME ANOTHER DAY!

Prayer: "Father, in making my plans, I seek the wisdom of counsel. Help me to listen and learn from others, integrating their perspectives into my vision. May my plans be strengthened and enriched by the diversity of opinions. Amen."

Reflection Question/Collaboration with God: "How can I integrate wise counsel into the pursuit of my vision?"

____

____

BEFORE GOING TO BED!

Evening Review: "How did I use the tips to refine my plans today?"

____

____

Thanks: "Thank you, Lord, for the wealth of advice and collective wisdom."

Notes for today or tomorrow:

____

____

Saturday - Divine Direction

Verse: Psalm 32:8 - "The Lord says, 'I will guide you along the best pathway for your life. I will advise you and watch over you.'"

THANK YOU GOD FOR GIVING ME ANOTHER DAY!

Prayer: "Lord, I rely on Your promise to instruct and guide me. As I pursue my vision, may I be attentive to Your counsel and responsive to Your guidance. May I walk with confidence, knowing that You have Your eye on me. Amen."

Reflection Question/Collaboration with God: "How can I remain open to God's guidance and instructions?"

____

____

BEFORE GOING TO BED!

Evening Review: "How did I perceive God's guidance and direction in my day?"

____

____

Thank You: "Thank You, Father, for Your constant presence and guidance in my life."

- Notes for today or tomorrow:

____

____

Sunday - Guided by the Lord

Verse: Psalm 37:23-24 - "The Lord directs the steps of the godly. He delights in every detail of their lives. Though they stumble, they will never fall, for the Lord holds them by the hand."

THANK YOU GOD FOR GIVING ME ANOTHER DAY!

Prayer: "Lord, I'm grateful that You strengthen my steps and delight in my path. In my quest for clear vision, support me in every challenge. Even if I stumble, I know You're there to pick me up. Guide me always in Your way. Amen."

Reflection Question/Collaboration with God: "How can I stay attentive to God's guidance and support as I pursue my vision?"

BEFORE GOING TO BED!

Evening Review: "How have I felt God's support in my moments of uncertainty or difficulty today?"

Thanks: "Thank You, Father, for Your kind hand that sustains and guides me."

Notes for today or tomorrow:

Week 6 (Sunday 6): Planning and preparation

Verse: Luke 14:28-30 -"But don't begin until you count the cost. For who would begin construction of a building without first calculating the cost to see if there is enough money to finish it? Otherwise, you might complete only the foundation before running out of money, and then everyone would laugh at you. They would say, 'There's the person who started that building and couldn't afford to finish it!'"

Reflection Question: "What are my key plans and preparations for the next week?"

Question to God: "What wisdom and resources do I need to ask God for in my planning and preparation?"

Gratitude Prayer: "Lord, thank You for the wisdom and clarity You bring to my planning. I'm grateful for the resources and opportunities You place in my path. Guide me as I build my projects. Amen."

Notes for the week ahead:

Monday - Diligence and Planning

Verse: Proverbs 21:5 - "Good planning and hard work lead to prosperity, but hasty shortcuts lead to poverty."

THANK YOU GOD FOR GIVING ME ANOTHER DAY!

Prayer: "Lord, inspire me to be diligent and thoughtful in my planning. May my efforts be guided by prudence to achieve abundance. Keep me from haste and guide me to thoughtful and effective actions. Amen."

Reflection Question/Collaboration with God: "How can I practice diligence in my planning today?"

____

____

BEFORE GOING TO BED!

Evening Review: "In what ways have I been diligent in my actions and planning today?"

____

____

Thanks: "Thank you, Father, for the wisdom that guides my plans toward abundance."

Notes for today or tomorrow:

____

____

Tuesday - Fulfillment of Plans

Verse: Psalm 20:4 - "May he grant your heart's desires and make all your plans succeed."

THANK YOU GOD FOR GIVING ME ANOTHER DAY!

Prayer: "Lord, You know my heart's desires and my plans. Help me to align my desires with Your will. May every step I take be guided by Your hand and lead to the fulfillment of Your purposes in my life. Amen."

Reflection Question/Collaboration with God: "How can my desires and plans align with God's will today?"

____

____

BEFORE GOING TO BED!

Evening Review: "How did I work toward the fulfillment of my plans with God's blessing today?"

____

____

Thank You: "Thank You, God, for Your support in bringing my plans to fruition."

Notes for today or tomorrow:

____

____

Wednesday - Pre-action preparation

Verse: Proverbs 24:27 - "Do your planning and prepare your fields before building your house."

THANK YOU GOD FOR GIVING ME ANOTHER DAY!

Prayer: "Father, guide me in the methodical preparation of my projects. May I be meticulous and organized in my preparations, ensuring a solid foundation before embarking on major projects. Help me to build with wisdom and foresight. Amen."

Reflection Question/Collaboration with God: "What essential preparations do I need to make today before taking action?"

____

____

BEFORE GOING TO BED!

Evening Review: "How effectively did I prepare the ground for my future actions today?"

____

____

Thanks: "Thank you, Lord, for the wisdom of preparation and the success it brings."

Notes for today or tomorrow:

____

____

Thursday - Responsibility and preparation

Verse: Luke 12:48 - "But someone who does not know, and then does something wrong, will be punished only lightly. When someone has been given much, much will be required in return; and when someone has been entrusted with much, even more will be required."

THANK YOU GOD FOR GIVING ME ANOTHER DAY!

Prayer: "Lord, I recognize the great responsibility entrusted to me. Help me to prepare myself adequately and to manage with wisdom and integrity all that You have entrusted to me. May I be faithful in the management of my resources and talents. Amen."

Reflection Question/Collaboration with God: "How can I faithfully respond to the responsibilities God has entrusted to me?"

____

____

BEFORE GOING TO BED!

Evening Review: "How did I manage my responsibilities and prepare my actions today?"

____

____

Thanks: "Thank You, God, for the trust You place in me and for the opportunities for growth."

Notes for today or tomorrow:

____

____

Friday - Divine foundation for projects

Verse: Psalm 127:1 - "Unless the Lord builds the house, the builders labor in vain. Unless the Lord watches over the city, the guards stand watch in vain."

THANK YOU GOD FOR GIVING ME ANOTHER DAY!

Prayer: "Father, may You be the foundation and guide of all my projects. I put my trust in You to build and protect what I undertake. May my efforts be aligned with Your will and led by Your hand. Amen."

Reflection Question/Collaboration with God: "How can I make sure my projects are based on God's principles and guidance?"

____

____

BEFORE GOING TO BED!

Evening Review: "In what ways have I integrated God into the foundation and progression of my projects today?"

____

____

Thank You: "Thank You, Lord, for Your guidance and protection in my endeavors."

Notes for today or tomorrow:

____

____

Saturday - Entrust your plans to God

Verse: Proverbs 16:3 - "Commit your actions to the Lord, and your plans will succeed."

THANK YOU GOD FOR GIVING ME ANOTHER DAY!

Prayer: "Lord, I entrust all my projects and plans to You. Direct my thoughts and actions so that my undertakings reflect Your glory and are carried out according to Your will. May every step I take be marked by Your blessing. Amen."

Reflection Question/Collaboration with God: "In what ways can I dedicate every aspect of my projects to God?"

BEFORE GOING TO BED!

Evening Review: "How did I see God working in the realization of my projects today?"

Thank You: "Thank You, Father, for the promise of success when I place my projects in Your hands."

Notes for today or tomorrow:

Sunday - Understanding the Value of Time

Verse: Psalm 90:12 - "Teach us to realize the brevity of life, so that we may grow in wisdom."

THANK YOU GOD FOR GIVING ME ANOTHER DAY!

Prayer: "Eternal Father, help me to understand and value each day You give me. May I be aware of the brevity of life and use my time wisely. Guide me to apply my heart to wisdom, planning and preparation that honor Your name. Amen."

Reflection Question/Collaboration with God: "How can I use my time today wisely and productively?"

BEFORE GOING TO BED!

Evening Review: "How did I apply wisdom in the use of my time today?"

Thanks: "Thank you, Lord, for the precious resource of time and for the wisdom to use it wisely."

Notes for today or tomorrow:

Week 7 (Sunday 7): Power of the Word

Verse: Hebrews 4:12 -"For the word of God is alive and powerful. It is sharper than the sharpest two-edged sword, cutting between soul and spirit, between joint and marrow. It exposes our innermost thoughts and desires."

Reflection Question: "How can I better understand and apply the power of God's Word in my life these next four weeks?"

Question to God: "What aspects of Your Word would I like God to illuminate for me during this time?"

Prayer of Gratitude: "Lord, thank You for Your living and powerful Word that guides and enlightens my path. Help me to apply it wisely and effectively to my life. May I be transformed and renewed by its truth. Amen."

Notes for the week ahead:

PS: I don't know if you've seen my book that might interest you "Why 1000X, is EASIER than 10X & SIMPLER than 2X!" English and French version on AMAZON!

Monday - Pleasant words

Verse: Psalm 19:14 - "May the words of my mouth and the meditation of my heart be pleasing to You, O LORD, my rock and my redeemer!"

THANK YOU GOD FOR GIVING ME ANOTHER DAY!

Prayer: "Lord, may my words and thoughts always be pleasing to Your eyes. Guide me to speak with wisdom and love, reflecting Your goodness in all I say and think. May I be an instrument of Your peace and truth. Amen."

Reflection Question/Collaboration with God: "How can my words and thoughts be a reflection of God's love and wisdom today?"

BEFORE GOING TO BED!

Evening Review: "In what ways have I used my words to honor God and bless others today?"

Thank You: "Thank You, Father, for the grace of being able to express words and thoughts that are pleasing to You."

Notes for today or tomorrow:

Tuesday - Life and Death in the Word

Verse: Proverbs 18:21 - "The tongue can bring death or life; those who love to talk will reap the consequences."

THANK YOU GOD FOR GIVING ME ANOTHER DAY!

Prayer: "Lord, help me to understand the immense power of my words. May I choose words that bring life and not death, that encourage and not discourage. May my words reflect Your love and truth. Amen."

Reflection Question/Collaboration with God: "In what ways can my words be a source of life and blessing today?"

____

____

BEFORE GOING TO BED!

Evening Review: "How did I use my words to positively influence others today?"

____

____

Thanksgiving: "Thank you, God, for the power of the word to bless and give life."

Notes for today or tomorrow:

____

____

Wednesday - Edifying words

Verse: Ephesians 4:29 - "Don't use foul or abusive language. Let everything you say be good and helpful, so that your words will be an encouragement to those who hear them."

THANK YOU GOD FOR GIVING ME ANOTHER DAY!

Prayer: "Father, may my words always be uplifting and gracious. Help me to speak in ways that strengthen others, bringing encouragement and wisdom. May I be a channel of Your grace through my words. Amen."

Reflection Question/Collaboration with God: "How can I make sure my words are constructive and kind today?"

____

____

BEFORE GOING TO BED!

Evening Review: "In what ways have I used my words to edify and encourage others today?"

____

____

Thank you: "Thank you, Lord, for the ability to use my words for the good and blessing of others."

Notes for today or tomorrow:

____

____

Thursday - Responsibility for words

Verse: Matthew 12:36-37 - "And I tell you this, you must give an account on judgment day for every idle word you speak. The words you say will either acquit you or condemn you."

THANK YOU GOD FOR GIVING ME ANOTHER DAY!

Prayer: "Lord, aware of the responsibility of every word spoken, help me to speak with wisdom and integrity. May I be careful and thoughtful, recognizing the impact of my words on myself and others. Amen."

Question for Reflection/Collaboration with God: "How can I be more mindful of the impact of my words today?"

____

____

BEFORE GOING TO BED!

Evening Review: "In what moments have I had to be particularly aware of the impact of my words today?"

____

____

Thanks: "Thank you, Father, for the wisdom to watch and measure my words."

Notes for today or tomorrow:

____

____

Friday - Listening, Speaking and Anger

Verse: James 1:19-20 - "Understand this, my dear brothers and sisters: You must all be quick to listen, slow to speak, and slow to get angry. Human anger does not produce the righteousness God desires."

THANK YOU GOD FOR GIVING ME ANOTHER DAY!

Prayer: "Lord, help me to be attentive and thoughtful in my communication. May I be quick to listen and measured in my words, avoiding anger that does not lead to Your justice. May my interactions reflect Your patience and understanding. Amen."

Reflection Question/Collaboration with God: "How can I practice active listening and thoughtful communication today?"

BEFORE GOING TO BED!

Evening Review: "How did I manage to be slow-talking and angry today?"

Thanks: "Thank you, Father, for teaching self-control in communication."

Notes for today or tomorrow:

Saturday -: Guard on the Lyrics

Verse: Psalm 141:3 -"Take control of what I say, O Lord, and guard my lips."

THANK YOU GOD FOR GIVING ME ANOTHER DAY!

Prayer: "Lord, I ask You to watch my words. May my mouth speak only words that are pleasing to You and that bless those around me. Protect me from saying impulsive or hurtful things. May my words be a reflection of Your wisdom and love. Amen."

Reflection Question/Collaboration with God: "How can I make sure my words are in line with God's values and love today?"

BEFORE GOING TO BED!

Evening Review: "In what ways have I been careful with my words today?"

Thank You: "Thank You, God, for the wisdom and restraint You bring to my word."

Notes for today or tomorrow:

Sunday - Words of Healing

Verse: Proverbs 12:18 - "Some people make cutting remarks, but the words of the wise bring healing."

THANK YOU GOD FOR GIVING ME ANOTHER DAY!

Prayer: "Lord, may my words be a remedy and not a sword. Help me to speak with gentleness and wisdom, bringing healing and comfort to those around me. May my tongue reflect Your compassion and grace. Amen."

Reflection Question/Collaboration with God: "How can my words bring healing and comfort to others today?"

BEFORE GOING TO BED!

Evening Review: "In what ways have I used my words to encourage and support others today?"

Giving thanks: "Thank you, God, for the gift of the word, which has the power to heal and restore."

Notes for today or tomorrow:

Week 8 (Sunday 8): Perseverance

Verse: Romans 5:3-5 - ""We can rejoice, too, when we run into problems and trials, for we know that they help us develop endurance. And endurance develops strength of character, and character strengthens our confident hope of salvation. And this hope will not lead to disappointment. For we know how dearly God loves us, because he has given us the Holy Spirit to fill our hearts with his love."

THANK YOU GOD FOR GIVING ME ANOTHER DAY!

Reflection Question: "What concrete actions can I take this week to demonstrate my perseverance?"

Question to God: "How can I stay motivated and focused on my goals despite the challenges?"

Prayer of Gratitude: "Father, thank You for Your strength and wisdom that guide me in my perseverance. Help me to remain determined and resolute in the pursuit of my goals. Amen."

Notes for the week ahead:

Monday - Reward for perseverance

-Verse: James 1:12 - "God blesses those who patiently endure testing and temptation. Afterward they will receive the crown of life that God has promised to those who love him."

THANK YOU GOD FOR GIVING ME ANOTHER DAY!

Prayer: "Lord, help me to endure trials and temptations patiently, knowing that the reward of Your promise awaits me. May my faith be strengthened through every trial, and may my love for You grow. Amen."

Question for Reflection/Collaboration with God: "How can I patiently face today's temptations and trials with faith?"

____

____

BEFORE GOING TO BED!

Evening Review: "How did I persevere in the face of today's challenges?"

____

____

Thanksgiving: "Thank you, Father, for the promise of the crown of life to those who persevere."

Notes for today or tomorrow:

____

____

Tuesday - Never Get Tired of Doing Well

Verse: Galatians 6:9 - "So let's not get tired of doing what is good. At just the right time we will reap a harvest of blessing if we don't give up."

THANK YOU GOD FOR GIVING ME ANOTHER DAY!

Prayer: "Lord, strengthen me so that I never tire of doing good. Help me to persevere in my righteous and charitable deeds, knowing that the reward will come in due time. May my heart remain committed to service and love. Amen."

Reflection Question/Collaboration with God: "How can I maintain my motivation to do good despite the challenges?"

BEFORE GOING TO BED!

Evening Review: "In what ways have I persevered in kindness and service today?"

Thanks: "Thank you, Father, for the strength to persevere in goodness and for the promise of the harvest to come."

Notes for today or tomorrow:

Wednesday - Constantly doing good

Verse: 2 Thessalonians 3:13 - "As for the rest of you, dear brothers and sisters, never get tired of doing good."

THANK YOU GOD FOR GIVING ME ANOTHER DAY!

Prayer: "Father, help me to remain diligent in doing good, whatever the circumstances. May I be an example of Your constancy and faithfulness by tirelessly pursuing works of charity and love. Amen."

Reflection Question/Collaboration with God: "What opportunities do I have today to continue doing good around me?"

____

____

BEFORE GOING TO BED!

Evening Review: "How have I contributed to the good of those around me today?"

____

____

Thank You: "Thank You, Lord, for the daily opportunities to reflect Your goodness."

Notes for today or tomorrow:

____

____

Thursday - Courage and hope

Verse: Psalm 31:24 -"So be strong and courageous, all you who put your hope in the Lord!"

THANK YOU GOD FOR GIVING ME ANOTHER DAY!

Prayer: "Lord, give me the strength and courage to persevere, especially in difficult times. May my heart be strengthened in the hope I have in You. May I bear witness to Your strength and faithfulness. Amen."

Reflection Question/Collaboration with God: "How can I strengthen my heart and mind to face today's challenges?"

____

____

BEFORE GOING TO BED!

Evening Review: "In what moments have I needed to draw on the strength and hope God offers me?"

____

____

Thank You: "Thank You, God, for the hope and courage You instill in my heart."

Notes for today or tomorrow:

____

____

Friday - Perseverance in Hope

Verse: Romans 12:12 - "Rejoice in our confident hope. Be patient in trouble, and keep on praying."

THANK YOU GOD FOR GIVING ME ANOTHER DAY!

Prayer: "Lord, in my times of tribulation, help me to remain joyful and hopeful. Strengthen my patience and perseverance. May I be diligent in prayer, seeking Your presence and guidance at all times. Amen."

Question for Reflection/Collaboration with God: "How can I stay focused on hope and prayer in the face of today's challenges?"

____

____

BEFORE GOING TO BED!

Evening Review: "How did I practice patience and find joy in hope today?"

____

____

Thanks: "Thank you, Father, for the joy and hope that sustain me in difficult times."

Notes for today or tomorrow:

____

____

Who do you think would find this book helpful and need to connect with God?

Know someone with untapped potential and God-given talents?

This book could be the key to unlocking their true capabilities.

Share it with them and help illuminate the path to their spiritual and personal growth.

____

____

____

____

____

____

https://1000xforthekingdom.com/12-weeks-10xfaith-and-contribution

Share the joy and connection with God with those people!

Saturday - Faith Run

Verse: Hebrews 12:1 - "Therefore, since we are surrounded by such a huge crowd of witnesses to the life of faith, let us strip off every weight that slows us down, especially the sin that so easily trips us up. And let us run with endurance the race God has set before us."

THANK YOU GOD FOR GIVING ME ANOTHER DAY!

Prayer: "Father, as I run the race of faith, help me to free myself from all that hinders me. May I remain focused and determined, moving forward with perseverance toward the goal You have set for me. Amen."

Reflection Question/Collaboration with God: "What burdens do I need to let go of to run the race of faith more efficiently?"

____

____

BEFORE GOING TO BED!

Evening Review: "How did I progress on my spiritual journey today?"

____

____

Thank You: "Thank You, Lord, for the strength and determination to follow the path You have laid out for me."

Notes for today or tomorrow:

____

____

Week 9-12 (Saturday 9): Vision and Goals

Verse: Philippians 2:3 - "Don't be selfish; don't try to impress others. Be humble, thinking of others as better than yourselves. Don't look out only for your own interests, but take an interest in others, too."

Reflection Question: "How can I use my leadership skills to positively influence those around me and reflect Christian values in my daily actions?"

Question to God: "Lord, how can I better serve and guide others while remaining faithful to Your teachings and ways?"

Gratitude Prayer: "Heavenly Father, thank You for the opportunities for growth and leadership You have placed in my path. Thank You for guiding me and giving me the wisdom to influence others with love, humility and integrity. Help me to be a reflection of Your light in this world. Amen."

What's your greatest achievement in the last 4 weeks? (I invite you to share it on social media by tagging me @KarlRoussel)

Notes for the next 4 weeks:

Sunday - Run to win

Verse: 1 Corinthians 9:24 - "Don't you realize that in a race everyone runs, but only one person gets the prize? So run to win!"

THANK YOU GOD FOR GIVING ME ANOTHER DAY!

Prayer: "Lord, inspire me to run life's race with the intention of winning. May every effort I make be guided by Your wisdom and purpose. Help me to stay disciplined, focused and committed to pursuing Your plans for my life. Amen."

Reflection Question/Collaboration with God: "How can I run this day's race with the goal of winning the heavenly prize?"

____

____

BEFORE GOING TO BED!

Evening Review: "In what ways have I aimed for excellence in my actions and faith today?"

____

____

Thank you: "Thank you, Father, for the motivation and stamina to run the race with perseverance and faith."

Notes for today or tomorrow:

____

____

Week 9 (Sunday 9): Servant leadership

Verse: Mark 10:45 - "For even the Son of Man came not to be served but to serve others and to give his life as a ransom for many."

Reflection Question: "What concrete actions can I take this week to serve others in my role as a leader?"

Question to God: "How can I practice humility and selflessness in my leadership this week?"

Gratitude Prayer: "Father, thank You for guiding me to be a leader who serves with love and humility. Inspire my actions and words to reflect Your servant love. Amen."

Notes for the week ahead:

Monday - Humility and Altruism

Verse: Philippians 2:3-4 - "Don't be selfish; don't try to impress others. Be humble, thinking of others as better than yourselves. Don't look out only for your own interests, but take an interest in others, too."

THANK YOU GOD FOR GIVING ME ANOTHER DAY!

Prayer: "Lord, help me to practice humility and prioritize the needs of others. May I be a leader who uplifts and supports others, setting aside selfishness and vanity. May my service reflect Your love and grace. Amen."

Reflection Question/Collaboration with God: "How can I focus on the needs and well-being of others today?"

____

____

BEFORE GOING TO BED!

Evening Review: "How did I practice humility and altruism in my interactions today?"

____

____

Thank you: "Thank you, Father, for the opportunity to serve others with humility and love."

Notes for today or tomorrow:

____

____

Tuesday - Service example

Verse: John 13:14-15 - "And since I, your Lord and Teacher, have washed your feet, you ought to wash each other's feet. I have given you an example to follow. Do as I have done to you."

THANK YOU GOD FOR GIVING ME ANOTHER DAY!

Prayer: "Lord Jesus, inspire me to follow Your example of humble and dedicated service. May I find ways to serve others with the same compassion and humility You have shown. Help me to be a leader who acts with love and consideration for others. Amen."

Question for Reflection/Collaboration with God: "How can I practice humble service in my daily life?"

BEFORE GOING TO BED!

Evening Review: "In what situations have I been able to serve others humbly and selflessly today?"

Thank You: "Thank You, Lord, for the perfect example of service You have established."

Notes for today or tomorrow:

Wednesday - Leadership by example

Verse: 1 Peter 5:2-3 - "Care for the flock that God has entrusted to you. Watch over it willingly, not grudgingly—not for what you will get out of it, but because you are eager to serve God. Don't lord it over the people assigned to your care, but lead them by your own good example."

THANK YOU GOD FOR GIVING ME ANOTHER DAY!

Prayer: "Heavenly Father, help me to guide and care for those in my charge with love and dedication. May I lead not out of compulsion or for personal gain, but in a spirit of service and by being a model of Your goodness and grace. Amen."

Reflection Question/Collaboration with God: "How can I be a model of servant leadership for those I lead?"

____

____

BEFORE GOING TO BED!

Evening Review: "How have I exercised leadership that reflects service and dedication today?"

____

____

Thank You: "Thank You, God, for the opportunity to serve and lead according to Your example."

Notes for today or tomorrow:

____

____

Thursday - Greatness in Service

Verse: Matthew 20:26-28 - "But among you it will be different. Whoever wants to be a leader among you must be your servant, and whoever wants to be first among you must become your slave. For even the Son of Man came not to be served but to serve others and to give his life as a ransom for many."

THANK YOU GOD FOR GIVING ME ANOTHER DAY!

Prayer: "Lord, may my desire for greatness be found in service to others. Help me to seek opportunities to serve rather than be served, reflecting Your sacrificial love and humility. May my life be a testimony to Your selfless service. Amen."

Reflection Question/Collaboration with God: "In what ways can I dedicate myself to serving others to reflect greatness in God's kingdom?"

____

____

BEFORE GOING TO BED!

Evening Review: "How have I put the principle of service to others into practice as a form of leadership today?"

____

____

Thank you, Father, for teaching us that true greatness is found in humble, loving service."

Notes for today or tomorrow:

____

Friday - Leading with Integrity and Wisdom

Verse: Psalm 78:72 - "So he cared for them with a true heart and led them with skillful hands."

THANK YOU GOD FOR GIVING ME ANOTHER DAY!

Prayer: "Lord, inspire me to lead with integrity of heart and great skill. May I be just, honest and wise in all my decisions. Help me to guide others with compassion and fairness, reflecting Your goodness and justice. Amen."

Reflection Question/Collaboration with God: "How can I practice integrity and wisdom in my role as a leader today?"

BEFORE GOING TO BED!

Evening Review: "In what ways did I demonstrate integrity and competence in my leadership today?"

Thank You: "Thank You, Father, for the wisdom and integrity You pour into my heart and actions."

Notes for today or tomorrow:

Saturday - Serving rather than dominating

Verse: Luke 22:26-27 - "But among you, it will be different. Those who are the greatest among you should take the lowest rank, and the leader should be like a servant. Who is more important, the one who sits at the table or the one who serves? The one who sits at the table, of course. But not here! For I am among you as one who serves."

THANK YOU GOD FOR GIVING ME ANOTHER DAY!

Prayer: "Lord Jesus, help me to adopt an attitude of service in my leadership. May I be willing to serve rather than dominate, to support rather than demand. May I follow Your example by being a servant to all. Amen."

Reflection Question/Collaboration with God: "In what concrete ways can I serve others in my role as a leader today?"

____

____

BEFORE GOING TO BED!

Evening Review: "How did I implement service in my leadership today?"

____

____

Thank You: "Thank You, Lord, for the perfect example of service You have established."

Notes for today or tomorrow:

____

Sunday - Gentle and Knowledgeable Leadership

Verse: 2 Timothy 2:24 - "A servant of the Lord must not quarrel but must be kind to everyone, be able to teach, and be patient with difficult people."

THANK YOU GOD FOR GIVING ME ANOTHER DAY!

Prayer: "Lord, give me the grace to lead with gentleness, to be teachable and patient in all my interactions. Help me to resolve conflicts with love and understanding, and to guide others to Your truth with wisdom. Amen."

Reflection Question/Collaboration with God: "How can I demonstrate gentleness, teachability and patience in my leadership today?"

____

____

BEFORE GOING TO BED!

Evening Review: "In what situations did I have to show patience and gentleness as a leader today?"

____

____

Thanks: "Thank you, Father, for the ability to lead with gentleness, patience and love."

Notes for today or tomorrow:

____

____

Week 10 (Sunday 10): Integrity and Honesty

Verse: Proverbs 11:3 - "Honesty guides good people; dishonesty destroys treacherous people."

Reflection Question: "How can I strengthen my integrity and sincerity in my relationships and actions?"

Question to God: "In what areas of my life do I need to be particularly vigilant this week to maintain my integrity?"

Gratitude Prayer: "Lord, thank you for inspiring and guiding me to act with honesty and integrity. May my actions be a faithful reflection of Your teachings. Amen."

Notes for the week ahead:

PS: I don't know if you've seen my book that might interest you "Why 1000X, is EASIER than 10X & SIMPLER than 2X!" English and French version on AMAZON!

Monday - Walking with Integrity

Verse: Proverbs 10:9 - "People with integrity walk safely, but those who follow crooked paths will be exposed."

THANK YOU GOD FOR GIVING ME ANOTHER DAY!

Prayer: "Father, guide me to walk constantly in integrity. Protect me from the temptation to take dishonest paths. May my conduct be blameless and transparent, bringing peace and security. Amen."

Reflection Question/Collaboration with God: "How can I ensure that my actions today are marked by unwavering honesty and integrity?"

____

____

BEFORE GOING TO BED!

Evening Review: "How did I demonstrate integrity in my actions and decisions today?"

____

____

Thanksgiving: "Thank you, Lord, for the security and peace that integrity brings to my life."

Notes for today or tomorrow:

____

____

Tuesday - The Truth in Words

Verse: Proverbs 12:22 - "The Lord detests lying lips, but he delights in those who tell the truth."

THANK YOU GOD FOR GIVING ME ANOTHER DAY!

Prayer: "Lord, may my words always be true and faithful. Help me to avoid lies and to speak with honesty, reflecting Your truthful nature. May my communication be pleasing in Your sight. Amen."

Reflection Question/Collaboration with God: "How can I make sure my words are sincere and faithful today?"

____

____

BEFORE GOING TO BED!

Evening Review: "How have I practiced honesty in my words and interactions today?"

____

____

Thanks: "Thank you, Father, for the gift of sincere and truthful communication."

Notes for today or tomorrow:

____

____

Wednesday - Surrender to the Lie

Verse: Ephesians 4:25 - "So stop telling lies. Let us tell our neighbors the truth, for we are all parts of the same body."

THANK YOU GOD FOR GIVING ME ANOTHER DAY!

Prayer: "Lord, help me to renounce falsehood and embrace truth in all my interactions. May I remember our interconnectedness and may my words contribute to unity and harmony. Amen."

Reflection Question/Collaboration with God: "In what ways can I practice truth in my relationships today?"

BEFORE GOING TO BED!

Evening Review: "How did I encourage unity and harmony through truth today?"

Giving thanks: "Thank you, God, for the bond of truth and unity we share as members of one another."

Notes for today or tomorrow:

Thursday - Living upright

Verse: Psalm 15:2 - "Those who lead blameless lives and do what is right, speaking the truth from sincere hearts."

THANK YOU GOD FOR GIVING ME ANOTHER DAY!

Prayer: "Father, may my life be a reflection of Your integrity and justice. Help me to be authentic in my actions and to speak the truth with love. May my conduct be a testimony to Your righteousness. Amen."

Reflection Question/Collaboration with God: "How can my daily life be an expression of integrity and righteousness?"

BEFORE GOING TO BED!

Evening Review: "In what situations have I had to stand firm in integrity and righteousness today?"

Thanksgiving: "Thank you, Lord, for the principles of justice and integrity that guide my life."

Notes for today or tomorrow:

Friday - Looking Straight Ahead

Verse: Proverbs 4:25-27 - "Look straight ahead, and fix your eyes on what lies before you. Mark out a straight path for your feet; stay on the safe path. Don't get sidetracked; keep your feet from following evil."

THANK YOU GOD FOR GIVING ME ANOTHER DAY!

Prayer: "Father, direct my eyes and my steps towards righteousness. Help me to stay focused on the path You have laid out for me, avoiding distractions and temptations. May I walk with integrity and honesty in all my actions. Amen."

Reflection Question/Collaboration with God: "How can I stay focused on a path of righteousness and integrity today?"

____

____

BEFORE GOING TO BED!

Evening Review: "In what ways have I managed to keep my eyes and steps aligned on the path of integrity?"

____

____

Thank You: "Thank You, Lord, for the clarity and direction You offer on life's journey."

Notes for today or tomorrow:

____

____

Saturday - Walking in Integrity

Verse: Proverbs 20:7 - "The godly walk with integrity; blessed are their children who follow them."

THANK YOU GOD FOR GIVING ME ANOTHER DAY!

Prayer: "Lord, may I be an example of integrity and righteousness. Help me to live in such a way as to leave a positive legacy for future generations. May my life be a reflection of Your truth and justice. Amen."

Reflection Question/Collaboration with God: "What legacy of integrity am I building for those who follow?"

____

____

BEFORE GOING TO BED!

Evening Review: "How have I embodied integrity in my life today, positively impacting those around me?"

____

____

Thanks: "Thank you, Father, for the opportunity to leave a legacy of righteousness and integrity."

Notes for today or tomorrow:

____

____

Sunday - Integrity and trust

Verse: Psalm 25:21 - "May integrity and honesty protect me, for I put my hope in you."

THANK YOU GOD FOR GIVING ME ANOTHER DAY!

Prayer: "Lord, may my hope in You guide me to a life of integrity and righteousness. Protect me from traps and errors, and help me to live in a way that honors Your name. May I trust in Your guidance and protection. Amen."

Reflection Question/Collaboration with God: "How can integrity and righteousness guide me in my choices and actions today?"

____

____

BEFORE GOING TO BED!

Evening Review: "In what ways have I demonstrated integrity and placed my trust in God today?"

____

____

Thank You: "Thank You, God, for the security and peace that comes from integrity and trust in You."

Notes for today or tomorrow:

____

____

Week 11 (Sunday 11): Positive Influence

Verse: Matthew 5:13-16 - "You are the salt of the earth. But what good is salt if it has lost its flavor? Can you make it salty again? It will be thrown out and trampled underfoot as worthless.
You are the light of the world—like a city on a hilltop that cannot be hidden.
No one lights a lamp and then puts it under a basket. Instead, a lamp is placed on a stand, where it gives light to everyone in the house.
In the same way, let your good deeds shine out for all to see, so that everyone will praise your heavenly Father."

Reflection Question: "In what ways can I be a positive influence and to be a light for others in my environment this week?"

Question to God: "How can I use my talents and abilities to positively impact my community and those around me?"

Gratitude Prayer: "Lord, thank you for giving me opportunities to positively influence others. Help me to use my gifts in ways that serve and encourage. Amen."

Notes for the week ahead:

Monday - Setting an example for others

Verse: 1 Timothy 4:12 - "Don't let anyone think less of you because you are young. Be an example to all believers in what you say, in the way you live, in your love, your faith, and your purity."

THANK YOU GOD FOR GIVING ME ANOTHER DAY!

Prayer: "Father, help me to be an example in my words and actions. May I show love, faith and purity in all I do. May my life inspire others to follow You and live according to Your principles. Amen."

Reflection Question/Collaboration with God: "In what ways can I be a model of faith and virtuous conduct today?"

____

____

BEFORE GOING TO BED!

Evening Review: "How have I been a positive example to others today?"

____

____

Thanks: "Thank you, Lord, for the opportunity to be a model for others in faith and love."

Notes for today or tomorrow:

____

____

Tuesday - Influence at any age

Verse: Psalm 71:18 - "Now that I am old and gray, do not abandon me, O God. Let me proclaim your power to this new generation, your mighty miracles to all who come after me."

THANK YOU GOD FOR GIVING ME ANOTHER DAY!

Prayer: "Lord, whatever my age, use me to positively influence the generations. May I share Your strength and wonders with young and old alike. Help me to pass on Your wisdom and love through my words and actions. Amen."

Reflection Question/Collaboration with God: "How can I share the experience of my faith with other generations today?"

BEFORE GOING TO BED!

Evening Review: "In what ways have I shared my spiritual experience with others today?"

Thanks: "Thank you, Father, for the wealth of experiences I can share with others."

Notes for today or tomorrow:

Wednesday - Shine like the stars

Verse: Philippians 2:15-16 - "so that no one can criticize you. Live clean, innocent lives as children of God, shining like bright lights in a world full of crooked and perverse people. Hold firmly to the word of life; then on the day of Christ's return, I will be proud that I did not run the race in vain and that my work was not useless."

THANK YOU GOD FOR GIVING ME ANOTHER DAY!

Prayer: "Lord, help me to live blameless and pure, shining like a star in this world. May my life be a clear testimony to Your grace and truth. Help me to hold fast to Your word of life in all circumstances. Amen."

Reflection Question/Collaboration with God: "In what ways can I reflect the light of Christ in my current environment?"

____

____

BEFORE GOING TO BED!

Evening Review: "How have I been a light in the world today?"

____

____

Thanksgiving: "Thank You, Lord, for the opportunity to illuminate this world with Your light."

Notes for today or tomorrow:

____

____

Thursday - Living with Awareness

Verse: 1 Peter 3:16 - "But do this in a gentle and respectful way. Keep your conscience clear. Then if people speak against you, they will be ashamed when they see what a good life you live because you belong to Christ."

THANK YOU GOD FOR GIVING ME ANOTHER DAY!

Prayer: "Father, may I always live with a clear conscience, acting with integrity and virtue. May those who may doubt or criticize see the truth and goodness of my life in Christ. Help me to be a living example of Your love. Amen."

Reflection Question/Collaboration with God: "How can I maintain a clear conscience in my interactions today?"

BEFORE GOING TO BED!

Evening Review: "How did I react to criticism or misunderstanding today with a clear conscience?"

Thanks: "Thank you, Father, for the peace that comes from a life lived with integrity and honesty."

Notes for today or tomorrow:

Friday - Wisdom in Interaction

Verse: Colossians 4:5-6 - "Live wisely among those who are not believers, and make the most of every opportunity. Let your conversation be gracious and attractive so that you will have the right response for everyone."

THANK YOU GOD FOR GIVING ME ANOTHER DAY!

Prayer: "Lord, grant me wisdom in my interactions, especially with those who don't know You. May my words be full of grace and appeal, revealing Your truth and love. Help me take every opportunity to share Your light. Amen."

Reflection Question/Collaboration with God: "How can I use my words to positively influence those around me today?"

BEFORE GOING TO BED!

Evening Review: "In what ways have I used wisdom and grace in my conversations today?"

Thanks: "Thank you, Father, for the ability to interact with wisdom and grace."

Notes for today or tomorrow:

Saturday - Be the Light of the World

Verse: Matthew 5:14 - "You are the light of the world—like a city on a hilltop that cannot be hidden."

THANK YOU GOD FOR GIVING ME ANOTHER DAY!

Prayer: "Father, help me to shine as a light in this world. May I not hide the light of Your presence within me, but illuminate it for all to see. May my life be a beacon of hope, truth and love. Amen."

Reflection Question/Collaboration with God: "In what ways can I be a visible light to the world today?"

____

____

BEFORE GOING TO BED!

Evening Review: "How have I reflected the light of Christ in my actions and words today?"

____

____

Thanksgiving: "Thank you, Lord, for the privilege and responsibility of being the light of the world."

Notes for today or tomorrow:

____

____

Sunday - Letters from Christ

Verse: 2 Corinthians 3:2-3 - "The only letter of recommendation we need is yourselves. Your lives are a letter written in our hearts; everyone can read it and recognize our good work among you. Clearly, you are a letter from Christ showing the result of our ministry among you, written not with ink but with the Spirit of the living God, not on tablets of stone but on human hearts."

THANK YOU GOD FOR GIVING ME ANOTHER DAY!

Prayer: "Lord, make my life a living letter of Christ. Let my existence bear witness to Your work in me. Write Your truth and love on my heart, and let my life be a proof of Your grace and salvation. Amen."

Reflection Question/Collaboration with God: "How can my life be a clear, legible letter that testifies to Christ's love and truth?"

____

____

BEFORE GOING TO BED!

Evening Review: "In what ways have I been a 'letter from Christ' in my interactions and witness today?"

____

____

Thank You: "Thank You, Father, for transforming me into a living letter, revealing Your love and truth."

Notes for today or tomorrow:

____

Week 12 (Sunday 12): Teamwork

Verse: Ecclesiastes 4:9-12 - "Two people are better off than one, for they can help each other succeed. If one person falls, the other can reach out and help.
But someone who falls alone is in real trouble. Likewise, two people lying close together can keep each other warm. But how can one be warm alone?
A person standing alone can be attacked and defeated, but two can stand back-to-back and conquer.
Three are even better, for a triple-braided cord is not easily broken."

THANK YOU GOD FOR GIVING ME ANOTHER DAY!

Reflection Question: "How can I improve my collaboration and teamwork in different aspects of my life?"

Question to God: "In what areas of my life do I need more collaboration and how can I be a better teammate?"

Gratitude Prayer: "Lord, thank you for the blessing of teamwork and community. Help me to recognize the value of sharing, mutual aid and unity in my efforts. May I be a support to others and know how to accept their help in return. Amen."

Notes for the week ahead:

Monday - United in Thought and Purpose

Verse: 1 Corinthians 1:10 - "I appeal to you, dear brothers and sisters, by the authority of our Lord Jesus Christ, to live in harmony with each other. Let there be no divisions in the church. Rather, be of one mind, united in thought and purpose."

THANK YOU GOD FOR GIVING ME ANOTHER DAY!

Prayer: "Father, unite us in our thoughts and goals. Help us to overcome divisions and work together for Your glory. May we speak with one voice, reflecting Your love and truth. Amen."

Reflection Question/Collaboration with God: "How can I contribute to unity and cohesion in my group or team today?"

BEFORE GOING TO BED!

Evening Review: "How did I promote unity and avoid divisions today?"

Thanks: "Thank you, Lord, for the gift of unity and brotherhood in Christ."

Notes for today or tomorrow:

Tuesday - One Body, Many Limbs

Verse: Romans 12:4-5 - "Just as our bodies have many parts and each part has a special function, so it is with Christ's body. We are many parts of one body, and we all belong to each other."

THANK YOU GOD FOR GIVING ME ANOTHER DAY!

Prayer: "Lord, help me to recognize and appreciate the diversity and uniqueness of each member of my team. May I work in harmony with others, valuing their unique contributions. Help us to function as a united body in Christ. Amen."

Reflection Question/Collaboration with God: "How can I better collaborate and value the unique talents of my team members?"

BEFORE GOING TO BED!

Evening Review: "How did I contribute to harmony and collaboration within my team today?"

Giving thanks: "Thank you, Father, for the diversity and unity we find in being members of one another."

Notes for today or tomorrow:

Wednesday - Serving with our Gifts

Verse: 1 Peter 4:10 - "God has given each of you a gift from his great variety of spiritual gifts. Use them well to serve one another."

THANK YOU GOD FOR GIVING ME ANOTHER DAY!

Prayer: "Father, thank You for the unique gifts You have placed in each of us. Help me to use my gifts to serve others, and to encourage my teammates to do the same. May we all be good stewards of Your graces. Amen."

Question for Reflection/Collaboration with God: "What gifts can I put at the service of my team to contribute effectively?"

____

____

BEFORE GOING TO BED!

Evening Review: "How did I use my talents and gifts to help and serve my team today?"

____

____

Thank you: "Thank you, Lord, for the opportunity to serve and be useful through my unique gifts."

Notes for today or tomorrow:

____

____

Thursday - Unity blessings

Verse: Psalm 133:1 - "How wonderful and pleasant it is when brothers live together in harmony!"

THANK YOU GOD FOR GIVING ME ANOTHER DAY!

Prayer: "Lord, may we find joy and sweetness in our unity and collaboration. Help us to appreciate the gift of brotherhood and to work together in love and harmony. May our unity be a source of blessing and encouragement. Amen."

Reflection Question/Collaboration with God: "How can I contribute to the atmosphere of unity and brotherhood in my work environment or community?"

BEFORE GOING TO BED!

Evening Review: "In what ways did I experience or foster unity within my team today?"

- Space for reply]

Thanks: "Thank you, Father, for the beauty and strength we find in fraternal unity."

Notes for today or tomorrow:

Friday - Every Member is Essential

Verse: 1 Corinthians 12:14-20 - "Yes, the body has many different parts, not just one part. If the foot says, 'I am not a part of the body because I am not a hand,' that does not make it any less a part of the body. And if the ear says, 'I am not part of the body because I am not an eye,' would that make it any less a part of the body? If the whole body were an eye, how would you hear? Or if your whole body were an ear, how would you smell anything? But our bodies have many parts, and God has put each part just where he wants it. How strange a body would be if it had only one part! Yes, there are many parts, but only one body."

THANK YOU GOD FOR GIVING ME ANOTHER DAY!

Prayer: "Lord, thank you for the diversity and uniqueness of each member in the body of Christ. Help me to recognize and value the importance of each person on my team. May we work together, understanding that everyone has an essential role to play. Amen."

Reflection Question/Collaboration with God: "How can I encourage and value the contributions of each member of my team?"

____

____

BEFORE GOING TO BED!

Evening Review: "How did I recognize and appreciate the diversity and unique talents within my team today?"

____

____

Thanksgiving: "Thank you, Lord, for the wisdom and beauty of diversity in unity."

1000XFORTHEKINGDOM.COM/10Xfaith-contribution-bonus

Saturday - Harmony and Solidarity

Verse: Philippians 2:1-2 - "Is there any encouragement from belonging to Christ? Any comfort from his love? Any fellowship together in the Spirit? Are your hearts tender and compassionate? Then make me truly happy by agreeing wholeheartedly with each other, loving one another, and working together with one mind and purpose."

THANK YOU GOD FOR GIVING ME ANOTHER DAY!

Prayer: "Father, inspire us to live in harmony and solidarity with one another. May we share the same love and spirit, working together for Your glory. Fill our hearts with tenderness and compassion. Amen."

Reflection Question/Collaboration with God: "In what ways can I promote harmony and solidarity within my team or community today?"

____

____

BEFORE GOING TO BED!

Evening Review: "How did I contribute to the cohesion and unity of my group today?"

____

____

Thanksgiving: "Thank you, Lord, for the joy of unity and harmony in the community."

Notes for today or tomorrow:

____

Sunday - Mutual sharpening

Verse: Proverbs 27:17 - "As iron sharpens iron, so a friend sharpens a friend."

THANK YOU GOD FOR GIVING ME ANOTHER DAY!

Prayer: "Lord, may our teamwork interactions sharpen and strengthen each other. Help us to learn from each other, grow together and encourage each other in our walk with You. Amen."

Reflection Question/Collaboration with God: "How can I contribute to the growth and improvement of my teammates today?"

BEFORE GOING TO BED!

Evening Review: "How did I help sharpen and strengthen my team's capabilities today?"

Thank you: "Thank you, God, for the enriching relationships that stimulate our growth and improvement."

Notes of the day

Take time to celebrate your accomplishment and thank GOD for his continued support during these 12 weeks!

What's your greatest achievement in the last 4 weeks? (I invite you to share it on social media by tagging me @KarlRoussel)

Join the Movement on 1000XForTheKingdom.com

Find out what's happening in our dynamic movement at: *__1000XForTheKingdom.com__*

We're in the middle of something, and your role is crucial. Together, we can achieve great things.

We are all part of our Savior's body, and every talent counts!

A Special Gift for You

To help you discover and harness your superpower, I've prepared a special gift that you'll find on the next page.

Take Action

Next 12-Week Season: Get ready to dive into a new season filled with growth and learning. Choose your next season in the store.

365 Days of Transformation: Embark on a year-long adventure to transform your life.

FREE GIFT for you!

Free PDF to find your unique talents
https://10xouicestpossible.com/3-steps-super-power

Indeed, we stand on the threshold of a great epic.

It's not an end, but a beginning.

It's the start of an epic journey that will take you to new heights. It's the start of an adventure that will change your life and the lives of many others.

Don't let your fear hold you back. Don't let your doubt crush you. Believe in yourself. Believe in your message. Believe in your potential.

Above all, act.

It's by taking action that you'll make your dreams come true.

I can't wait to see you shine. I can't wait to see you succeed. I can't wait to see you realize your dreams.

Now, with this book in your hands, you have a better understanding of your ideal customer.

Your self-confidence is strengthened and your process is clearer than ever.

That's the next step.

Maybe you're wondering what's after the book.

There are online training courses you can buy to help you.

But the aim is to push you to see something bigger.

My philosophy is to encourage people to live the life they were meant to live.

It frustrates me to see people living below their potential. We all have immense potential within us, an incredible contribution we can make.

I invite you to open yourself to that. This is you.
I'm not saying this to flatter your ego.

You'll have to work hard to get there. Even if you decide to work with us, invest all your means to get a coach and join the Maxime Propulsion program, it will be useless if you don't become the person you're meant to be.

I'm telling you this because I care about you.

Because I believe in your potential and that you have what it takes to become that person. If you feel diminished, it's not me who's put you down, it's you.

I encourage you to look upwards. Now's the time to raise your head and go for it with your book, an extremely powerful tool.

Thanks to this book, you'll understand who you are and why you should be proud of yourself. You'll also understand your process and why you're the best person to carry it out.

We're at an incredible moment in history.

Access to information, technology, artificial intelligence and resources are all within our reach.

There's never been a better time to be an entrepreneur, to be an author, to share your message and make a meaningful contribution.

If you're worried about artificial intelligence taking over all the work and recognition of humans, let me share with you a thought I had on my end-of-day walk some time ago: It'
s the entrepreneurs with high emotional intelligence who will get the most out of artificial intelligence!

This is the time to focus on what matters most: your vision, your goal, your dreams.

You can't hide behind excuses anymore.

And if you're feeling overwhelmed, remember, you don't have to have all the answers right away.

It's simply a matter of taking one step at a time.

The important thing is to keep moving forward, learning, growing, evolving. It's time to leave your mark on the world.

So, what do you decide?

Are you going to let this opportunity pass you by without taking action?

Will you continue to underestimate yourself, to limit yourself, to put yourself down?

Or will you stand up, take your place and become the leader you're destined to be?

Don't wait for a perfect moment.
There is no perfect moment.

Only now.

It's time to act, to take control of your destiny.

It's time to push yourself, to show courage, determination and resilience.

It's time to realize that you're unique, that you have a valuable message to share and that you can make a significant contribution to the world. So seize this opportunity.

Use this book as a springboard to propel you forward.

1000XFORTHEKINGDOM.COM/10Xfaith-contribution-bonus

Let your light shine.

Always remember that you are the best person to carry your message.

No one can do it with more passion, authenticity and dedication than you.

Be bold. Be brave. Be yourself.

I encourage you to move forward, to believe in yourself, to believe in your dreams. The world needs you.

The world needs your voice.

Talk. Write. Share. Inspire.

Because :

You're enough

And with GOD by your side, even more so!

GO to 1000XForTheKingdom.com me to get MORE impact, freedom and FUN in your business and your life.

Where 1000X rhymes with REVOLUTION!

Congratulations, you've completed your first reading!
Now, share this experience with your network.

Take a photo of yourself with this book and share what you liked best.

You could inspire others to create more impact, freedom and FUN in their lives!

What a perfect time to make a first announcement about your own upcoming book project...

And don't forget to tag me @KarlRoussel so I can encourage you on your journey.

**BONUS MEGA: One-to-One Proximity Coaching

Personal Coaching with Me: As a MEGA BONUS, I'm offering you the chance to benefit from one-to-one coaching.

HOW to access it without investing $€? Share Your Revelation: Take a photo with the book, write down your biggest revelation of the last 12 weeks thanks to this guide and TAG me!

Win a Coaching: Every month, 3 people will have the chance to win a 30-minute coaching session worth $2,500US with me.

WHO is Karl Roussel?

It's time for competent, well-meaning coaches to transform more lives, generate more income and move to the next level of abundance.

My name is Karl Roussel, MAXIMI$€UR of GROWTH and servant of GOD.

Passionate about business, sales, Jesus, the relationship with money, but above all about people, I've always enjoyed discussing subjects that we use every day.

Why bury your head in the sand when you're selling all the time and using money every day?

Over the past few years, I've made rapid progress in the field of entrepreneurship.

As a MAXIMI$AT€UR of potential, speaker, buying inspirer (closer), and creator of the MAXIMI$€ and GO "shoot" for the million! movement, I'm determined to help others achieve more and have more fun.

I used a high-level human skill (buying inspiration) to take control of my life and sell ethically and humanely.
Now I want to help you do the same.

Join Me on Social Media!

I'm glad you chose to read this book, and I'm even more excited to continue this adventure with you beyond these pages.

To stay connected, I invite you to join me on social media. You'll find not just enriching and motivational content, but also a community of individuals who, like you, are determined to unlock their next level for more freedom, impact, and fun!

Facebook: Join the Facebook group: 1000X REVOLUTION at https://www.facebook.com/groups/why1000xrevolution

Instagram: For inspiring moments of reflection, tips, and advice. https://www.instagram.com/karlroussel/

YouTube: Where you can find a variety of training and inspirational videos to help you on your entrepreneurial journey. https://www.youtube.com/karlroussel

TikTok: For quick motivational moments, real-time advice, and a glimpse into my daily life as an entrepreneur. @karlroussel

LinkedIn: For more professional content and networking opportunities.
https://www.linkedin.com/in/karl-roussel-7b32b434/

And finally, don't forget to subscribe to my podcast, "WHY 1000X!", where I share stories and reflections, interviews, and strategies to help entrepreneurs like you reach a million.

Looking forward to seeing you online!

NOT your copy of my new book yet? WHY is 1000X Easier than 10X and Simpler Than 2X?

TAKE your copy in French or English of my revolutionary book:

Now go to:

1000XREVOLUTION.COM

1000XFORTHEKINGDOM.COM/10Xfaith-contribution-bonus

When it comes to the "three M's" (Maximize, Multiply, Momentum) the foundations of 1000X REVOLUTION :

MAXIMI$€:

Inspired by the story of Samuel in 1 Samuel 3, where young Samuel hears God's call despite his tender age.

"The Lord called Samuel, who answered, 'Here I am!' He ran to Eli and said, 'Here I am, for you called me.'

But Eli replied, 'I didn't call; go back to bed.' Samuel went to bed. [...]

The Lord called Samuel again.

Samuel got up, went to Eli and said, 'Here I am, for you called me.' Eli replied, 'I did not call, my son; go back to bed.' [...]

The Lord called Samuel for the third time. [...] Eli understood that it was the LORD who was calling the child."

This story illustrates the importance of assuming God's call and using the talents He has already placed in our hearts, all that remains is for us to MAXIMI$€R it by multiplying it with momentum, whatever our age or situation.

Multiply :

2 Corinthians 9:10, "He who provides seed for the sower and bread for his food will provide for you and multiply your seed, and increase the fruits of your righteousness."

We emphasize that multiplying our resources and gifts is a natural extension of our faith.

As servants of Christ, we are called to extend the impact of our faith and service.

Momentum :

Galatians 6:9, "Let us not grow weary in doing good, for we will reap in due season if we do not slacken."

This verse reminds us not to grow weary of doing good, because perseverance in faith and good works creates a spiritual momentum that propels us towards a richer, more committed life.

May this book be a tool to enrich the spiritual life of each of you, and to help your community grow in faith and love for God and for others.

With my best thoughts and prayers,

Karl Roussel

In praise of Why 1000X? and Karl Roussel!

Karl Roussel, a man of God with a global vision, has an exceptional talent for mentoring individuals to MAXIMI$€ their potential.
His passion for spiritual growth and his ability to inspire are vividly evident throughout the pages of his daily guide.

Patricia Bartell, CEO, Crush It On Stage

Karl's desire to see you grow and MAXIMI$€ your innate potential 1000 times over shines through in his positive, faith-based personality.
He loves to challenge everyone to grow exponentially and provides you with the next steps to make it a reality.

Debra Savage Founder of 90 Days of Financial Clarity

Karl's relentless vision of everyone becoming a millionaire is infectious, and made me believe I really could!

Garrett Fromme, CEO, IDC Woodcraft

Karl's book simply digs inside what most business owners don't pay enough attention to: MAXIMI$€ their potential!
This short, magic word is the key to success and failure in any business model.

Germano Dealessandri, CEO and noise pollution management/problem-solving expert

Karl has a unique ability to help people sell themselves, their services or their products with confidence.

Martin Latulippe, speaker, author,
Coach and founder of the Zero Limits Academy

Karl is a true MAXIMI$€ and this book will help you reach your MAXIMI$€ potential. He openly shares his techniques and has done so many times.

has also helped me. Sometimes the biggest obstacle to a person's success is the way they see and deal with the situation. Karl helps point the way.

Dev Sethi, CEO of Wealth On Command and winner of the Global Sales Champion award

It's an immense privilege to have been able to grow personally and professionally with a coach whose heart is as big as the world. Thank you Karl Roussel for everything you've given me and for everything you ARE!

Dominique Samson, Training Consultant

I worked with Karl on the same team, and his discipline and consistency in closing deals drove me forward just by watching him.

Angelo D'Acunto, founder of Premium Closer

Karl has an innate gift that's hard to explain! Everything is possible for real! Having worked with him for over a year, I can say that he has equipped me for the long haul! Thank you Karl.

Karine Labrie, General Manager of Mdame Kay ; Ici & Maintenant sans filtre INC.

When you think you're at the top of your game in your business, but you can go further with a little help. That's what coach Karl Roussel helped me develop.

Mélanie Drouin, founder of the Institut d'Esthétique Mélanie Drouin

Karl is a true catalyst for success.
With his do-it-yourself mindset, lightning-fast solutions and direct, energizing approach, he's an absolute game-changer for coaches seeking exponential growth.

Sylvia Silvers, CEO, Sylvia Silvers Academy

www.ingramcontent.com/pod-product-compliance
Lightning Source LLC
Chambersburg PA
CBHW070131260726
48658CB00001B/358